# Crypto Investing

# Price Action Concepts

# A Comprehensive Guide for Beginners

By: Daviid Mouscho

# Contents

# Introduction

This book was written to give the reader an understanding of what is called price action in terms of trading. The term is applicable to all types of markets that include indices, forex and crypto currency. Price action is what you see on a chart and is made up of buys and sells in the market.

The concepts discussed in the book have been written to help the reader to understand them and utilise them in their own strategy.

Price action is a trading strategy that focuses on analyzing and making decisions based on the actual price movements of an asset rather than relying on traditional indicators and technical analysis tools.

# Price Action Concepts

Price Action

Price action is the movement of a security's price plotted over time. Price action forms the basis for all technical analysis on any asset's chart. Many short-term traders rely exclusively on price action and the patterns from it to make trading decisions.

Technical analysis as a practice is a derivative of price action since it uses past prices in calculations that can then be used to make informed trading decisions.

Price action can be seen and interpreted using charts that plot prices over time. Traders use different chart compositions to improve their ability to spot and interpret trends, breakouts, and reversals.

Many traders use candlestick charts since they help better visualize price movements by displaying the open, high, low, and close values in the context of up or down sessions.

Candlestick patterns are examples of visually interpreted price action.

Price action is not generally seen as a trading tool like an indicator, but rather the data source off which all the tools are built. Indicators lag, price action leads.

Swing traders and trend traders tend to work most closely with price action, eschewing any fundamental analysis in favour of focusing solely on support and resistance levels to predict movements.

Even these traders must pay some attention to additional factors beyond the current price, as the volume of trading and the time periods being used to establish levels all have an impact on the likelihood of their interpretations being accurate.

Throughout your trading career you will find which confluence factors you find the most useful to implement in your strategies.

Interpreting price action is very subjective. You need two participants to have a valid market, one side must be willing to sell and the other must be willing to buy, and each side will have its own reasons to do so.

It's common for two traders to arrive at different conclusions when analyzing the same price action. One trader may see a bearish downtrend, and another might believe that the price action shows a potential near term turnaround. Of course, the timeframe being used also has a huge influence on what traders see as a stock can have many intraday downtrends while maintaining a higher timeframe uptrend.

The important thing to remember is that trading predictions made using price action on any time scale are speculative.

The more tools you can apply to your trading hypothesis to confirm it, the better, this is what traders call confluence. In the end, however, the past price action of a security is no guarantee of future price action.

High probability trades are still speculative trades, which means traders take on risks to get access to potential rewards.

Now, let's define some basic price action concepts and shed some light on how to interpret and execute them properly.

# Ranges

Ranges are the zones where price consolidates after a time of trending price action. After an expansive move, you start looking for ranges to form.

To find them you need to wait for the pump/dump to end and then you proceed to firstly mark the first swing high / first swing low, then mark the first swing low / first swing high.

This may not be perfect at first, this is why you need to be redrawing them to gain the most confluence.

The range must be established where the majority of swing highs and lows are; you are looking for the majority of points of contact.

The EQ (equilibrium level) mark also must make sense

How does price behave around it?

Is it an area of reaction?

> Candles closing above the EQ = bullish
> Candles closing below the EQ = bearish

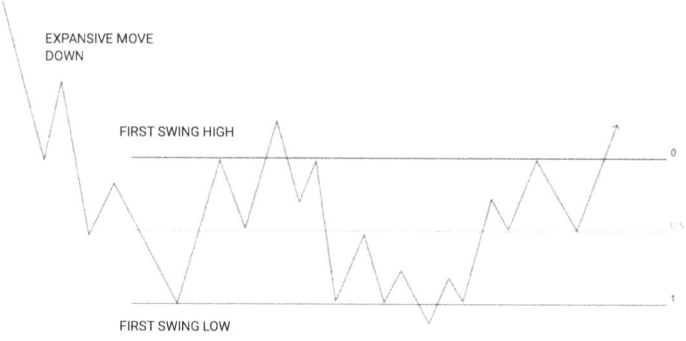

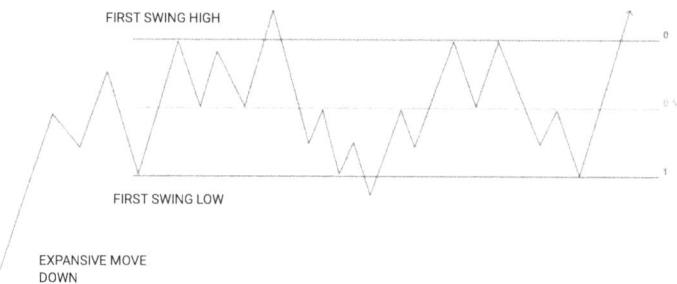

As you can see, there is no golden rule when it comes to drawing ranges. Most of the times you'll find yourself redrawing them until you find what makes the most sense.

Flipping Ranges Setup

For both macro and micro ranges, their ceilings/bottoms represent areas of high interest to the market. This is where the Flipping Ranges Setup comes to light. It's basically a S/R flip you can spot by extending the levels of previously broken ranges.

You need to consider that time + Space is key, just as in a S/R flip, the more time and space elapses before a retest = higher probabilities to succeed.

This can also happen near to HTF levels (adding confluence is key), an untested SSR often offers high-probability setups.

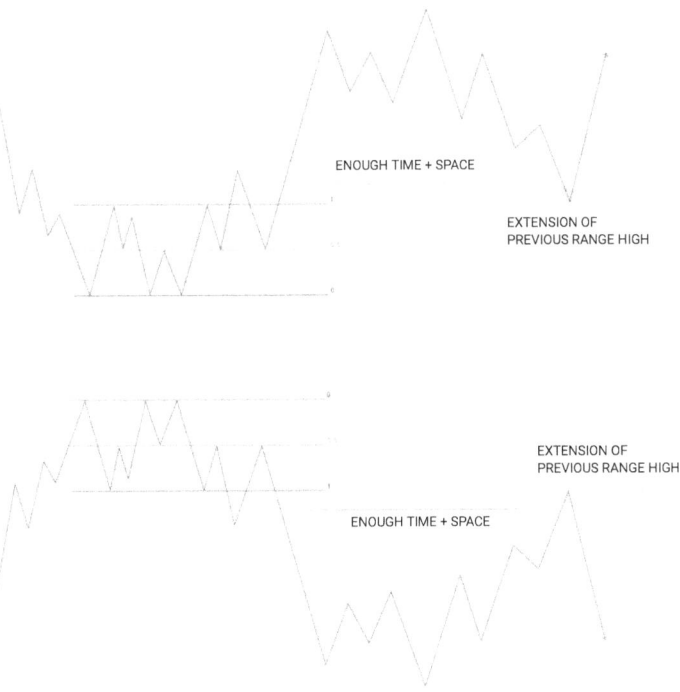

Ranges tend to offer high-strike plays as long as we can keep up with structure and recent price action. With some basic approaches like:

The market is always looking for liquidity, and most of the time it bounces between the areas where it finds it, before making an expansive move (ranges are formed under this premise).

It is a fact that markets only trend around 30% of the time, while ranging the most of it (this is probably a made-up statistic, but it works).

When playing Ranges Effectively, anticipate the formation of the range and redraw constantly until it makes sense. All levels in a range represent reaction areas, watch your trades if price comes near these levels such as range highs and range lows, including EQ.

Make sure price has collected liquidity before making moves and don't get trapped in a short squeeze for example. The ranges allow you to flip bias constantly, since there isn't a clear HTF trend.

There are probability enhancers such as directional bias market structure, Patterns and MSB Setups.

Trading in tandem with HTF structure assures you are not counter-trend trading. Trades in the same direction as HTF market structure are high probability plays.

Avoid breakout trading, violent moves may occur to trigger stops at the extremes of the range and be aware of HTF S/D zones, price may look for liquidity in those areas before coming back to the range.

Follow this mantra until the range is invalidated:

Bullish/cautious at the lows

Bearish/cautious at the highs

SWING LOW FORMS

RANGE FLIPPED

SWING LOW FORMS

LIQ GRAB II

LIQ GRAB III

THIS WAS ALSO A THREE TAP SETUP

# Market Structure

Market structure allows you to determine the flow of the market, for the most of traders it determines the trend direction. Market structure allows you to be in sync with the market and avoid counter-trend trading, which enhances the probability of your setups.

There are three stages in the market:

1. Uptrend - Series of higher highs followed by higher lows.

2. Ranges – Series of highs and lows within a specified range.

3. Downtrend - Series of lower highs followed by lower lows.

*Remember, the market only trends around 30% of the time. The remaining 70% it ranges.*

Example of an uptrend with a series of higher highs and higher lows.

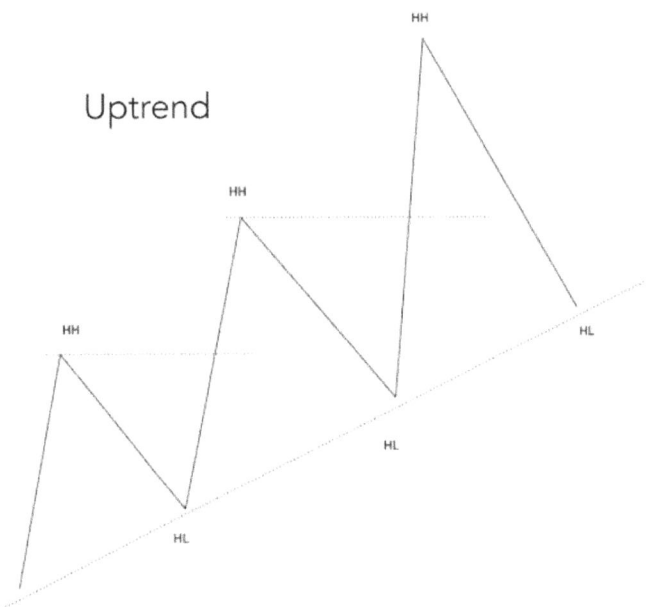

Example of a downtrend with a series of lower highs followed by lower lows

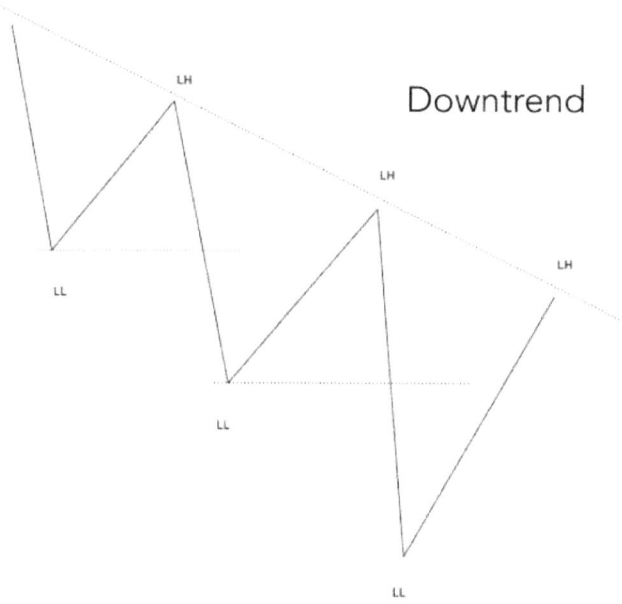

Downtrend

What is a range? As previously explained, a range is where price finds itself bouncing between two clear levels (range highs and range lows).

After a trending period price usually will re-accumulate or distribute through a period of ranging.

For an uptrend to stay intact, it must preserve its ascending structure. Higher lows must be followed by higher highs. Lower highs are allowed as price starts to compress, or manifest re-accumulation patterns, In the case of a downtrend, these are governed by their series of lower highs.

It remains intact as long as no lower high is broken. Higher lows are allowed as they may be re-distribution patterns.

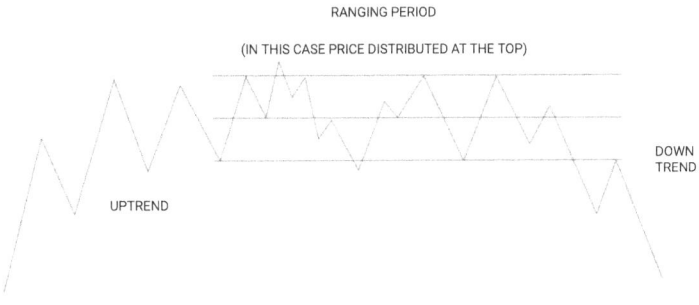

# Market Structure Break

A market structure break or MSB can easily tell us when the market has shifted from one trend to another. It allows us to plan our setups in the same direction as the trend.

how we can effectively tell if the market structure has been broken and to avoid being caught in a fake MSB.

For an upside MSB to occur price must close above the previous lower-high wick a. Beware of SFP's which will be explained later on.

For a downside MSB to occur price must close below the previous higher-low wick and again, beware of SFP's.

*Don't over complicate what constitutes a valid proper higher-low or a proper lower-high, as you begin to chart use the most obvious, to the market structure and you'll be more than fine.*

Market structure break (MSB) to the downside. Price shifted an uptrend to a downtrend.

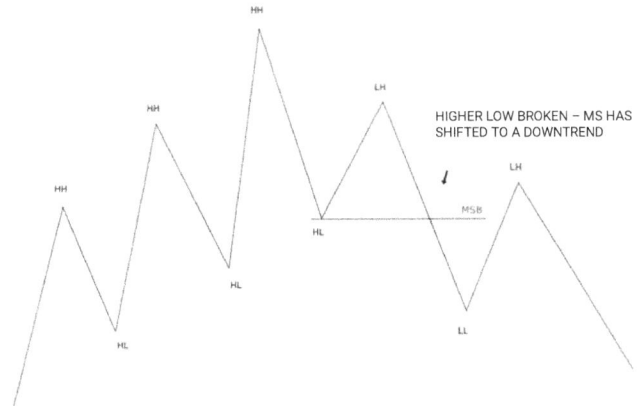

Market structure break (MSB) to the upside. Price shifted a downtrend to an uptrend.

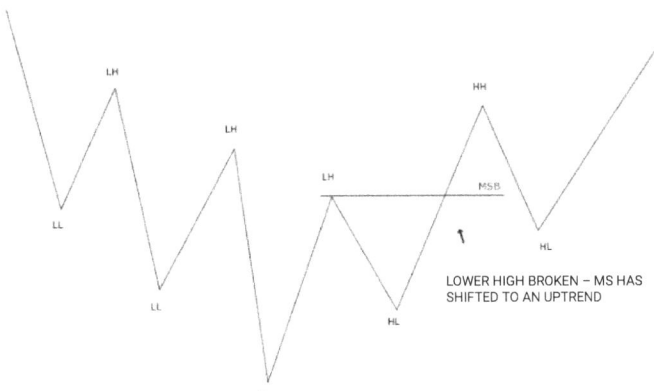

Criteria for a Lower High to be Valid, it must be a swing high.

A higher wick in-between two lower candles and it must lead to a new or equal low.

Criteria for a Higher Low to be Valid, it must be a swing low.

A lower wick in-between two higher candles and it must lead to a new or equal high.

HIGHER LOW

To anticipate future price action, watch how the current structure is developing, if in an uptrend for example Is price making higher lows but failing to print higher highs? Those are signs of compression.

COMPRESSION

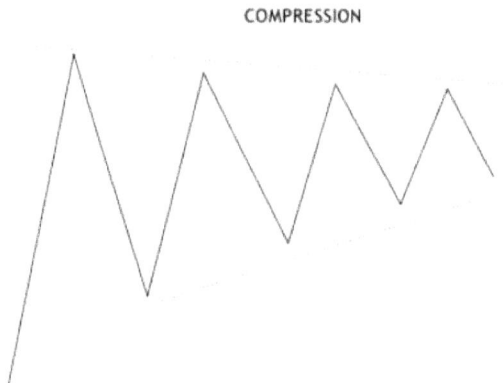

Is price struggling to print higher lows while making subsequent lower highs, then this is potential signs of reversal.

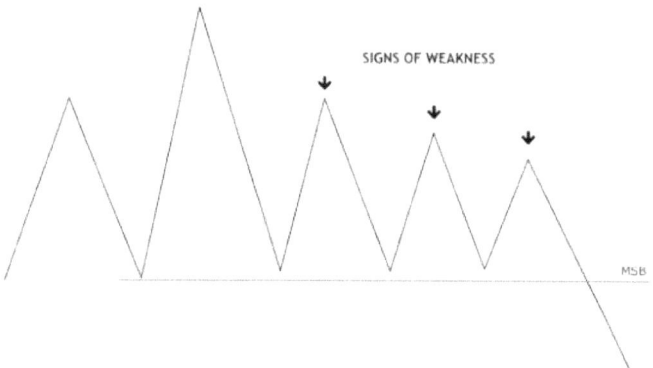

If in a downtrend for example, is price making lower highs but failing to print lower lows, then those are signs of compression.

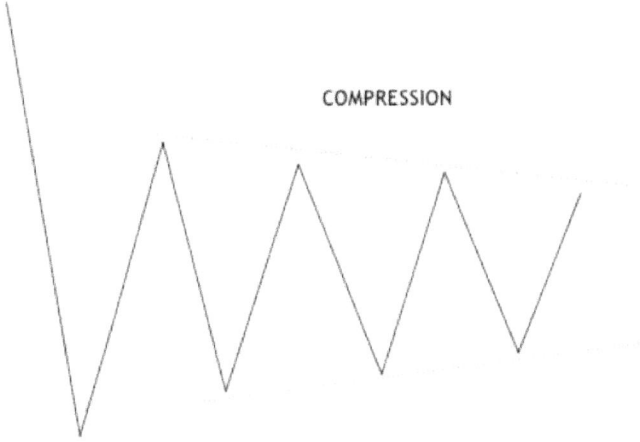

Is price making subsequent higher lows, then this is potential signs of reversal

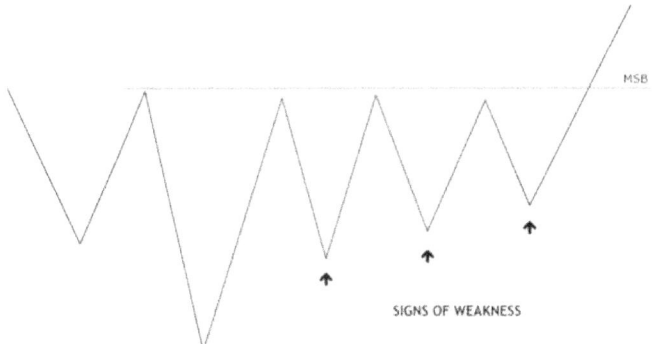

## Support and Resistance

These are pivotal zones to the market. Whether it is a psychological level, or some area derived from a Fibonacci extension, these areas represent high-interest prices to the market. Therefore, you can anticipate reactions from them.

I don't consider S/R as a reliable strategy by its own, but being aware of where they are located adds confluence to your ideas.

Order blocks found at S/R levels give high-probability setups, this allows you to play S/R flips more effectively and Over-and-Unders can be found at these levels as well.

It's all about enhancing the probability of your setups, and S/R areas surely offer some help to it.

SSR RETEST + RANGE
FLIP=HIGH PROB SETUP 8%
REACTION FROM THE LOWS

Notes:

Consolidation above support is bearish
Consolidation below resistance is bullish

Similar to support and resistance, we have the following concepts:

First Obstacle (FO)
Supply and Demand Clusters

All of these offer actionable areas and potential plays as long as we are acting in tandem with our strategy and count with sufficient confluence. Don't try to be a hero and predict a top/bottom, follow the trend and avoid getting stopped out.

# Supply and Demand

The difference between resistance/support and supply/demand is that supply and demand tend to be fresh untouched areas of interest that can potentially provide short term liquidity (price power) to temporarily give the market a reversal.

As for resistance/support, they represent historical pivot price lines that have played a crucial point in previous price outlining. We spot supply and demand zones through order blocks.

Order blocks constitute supply and demand areas in a visual way. They offer precise entries and easy invalidation levels; therefore, they are a fundamental pillar to price action trading.

But fundamentally speaking, order blocks are zones in which price denotes a level of interest, as its name states: collective/group of orders can be found in them. In order blocks, liquidity is injected to be used at a future time, therefore the reaction from them is usually aggressive.

An order block is a down or up candle near a key level that preceded an impulsive move up or down.

In the example below you can see a bullish order block is a down candle near a support level that preceded an impulsive move up.

MSB

FORMED DEMAND

BULLISH OB: LAST DOWN CANDLE
BEFORE IMPULSIVE MOVE DOWN

In the example below you can see the bearish order block is an up candle at/near a resistance level that preceded an impulsive the move down.

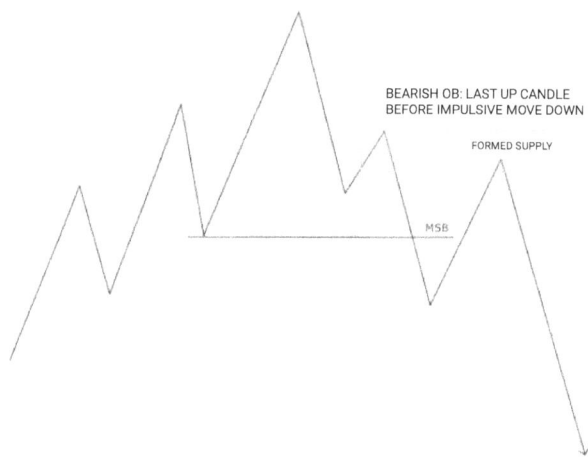

But not all order blocks are tradeable order blocks. We can use the following criteria to help ascertain if an order block is valid.

For an Order block to be valid, it should be located near a HTF support or resistance level (at least on a directional TF).

The order block must precede a break in market structure and the imbalance preceded by the order block must be two times the OB (magnitude of reaction)

The order block must take out an opposing order block, this increases the interest in the level.

To help identify Bullish Order blocks, ensure that HTF M.S. (according to your timeframe matrix) is bullish (explained at the end of the doc) and start looking for areas of interest in your directional bias (S/R levels).

Then drill down to your entry TF and begin to look for order blocks around those levels. A bullish OB is identified as the last down candle before the impulsive move up.

It has to fit the definition, once it meets the basic criteria you validate it with the characteristics stated above.

To help identify Bearish Order blocks, ensure that HTF M.S. (according to your timeframe matrix) is bearish (explained at the end of the doc) and start looking for areas of interest in your directional bias (S/R levels).

Then drill down to your entry TF and begin to look for order blocks around those levels. A bearish OB is identified as the last up candle before the impulsive move down.

It has to fit the definition, once it meets the basic criteria you validate it with the characteristics stated above.

But this isn't as easy it seems; the validity of the OB is key to its execution. Let's add some visual examples and further develop on the criteria.

What makes this Order block valid?

30k is a SSR for Bitcoin, which makes it a high-interest level, it was the last down candle before the impulsive move up that broke market structure.

The rally (imbalance) away from the OB is larger than 2x the OB, which adds tremendous interest to the OB Once it meets the validity criteria, we look forward to executing it.

Valid Order block:

VISUALLY, THIS IS HOW IT SHOULD LOOK.
LAST DOWN CANDLE BEFORETHE
IMPULSIVE MOVE UP

Invalid Order block:

IT CETAINLY IS THE LAST DOWN CANDLE BEFORE THE MOVE UP, IS IT VALID? NO.

What invalidates this Order block?

Even though it fulfils most of the criteria, the OB isn't the last down candle before the impulsive move up. As you can see, in the next candle price went lower than our marked-out OB, this automatically invalidates the OB. However, there certainly was a rally after that down candle, so we proceed to do the following:

Drill down to LTF to find the correct OB that preceded the move and mark it out. This was on CRV/USD 1D Chart, so we proceed in the following order:

1. 12h

2. 8-6h

3. 4h

We drilled all the way down to the 6H chart until we found the correct Order block. It previously met most of the criteria, but it was invalidated due to the lower wick in the following candle.

30

VALID H6 DEMAND

LAST DOWN CANDLE BEFORE
THE IMPULSIVE MOVE UP

Now that we found ourselves a proper Order block, the next question is: how to execute them?

Our order block should contain a considerable number of orders waiting to be filled. If the order block is valid then price shouldn't be able to go lower than our marked-out zone. Therefore, here is one conservative way to play Order blocks:

Bullish OB: entry at the top of the OB, invalidation below the lowest price of the OB then target next swing highs / liquidity areas.

Bearish OB: entry at the bottom of the OB, invalidation above the highest price of the OB then target next swing lows / liquidity areas.

This is how we would wait for price to retrace with our limit orders set.

How can we avoid bidding/asking invalid Order blocks?

You could have marked out a valid order block. However, that doesn't guarantee you that price will respect it.

No strategy has a 100% strike rate and order blocks aren't the exception.

General market conditions and previous price action are key to determine if we should be entering our trades on aggressive or conservative entries.

One of the most recommended things to do is to monitor LTF price action as price approaches our area of interest.

If price is showing bullish price action patterns, that increases the probabilities of the demand order block to be valid, and the opposite is true for supply order blocks. If we detect these patterns, then we look forward to entering our positions.

If the OB fails as a Supply/Demand block that turns it into a breaker of the opposite nature, we will develop on those later.

Remember for all the previously mentioned points for bullish order blocks, the opposite is true for Bearish Order blocks.

When choosing what timeframe to look for OBs there is technically no right or wrong way to mark-out an OB, but you want it as close to the MSB as possible and the stronger the move away from the level, the better the Supply/Demand OB.

The less time spent at the level, the better the supply/demand OB because it is often, you will likely get overlapping OB/breakers within multiple timeframes.

When trading overlapping OBs

LTF OBs = good for optimal entries with higher Risk Reward

HTF OBs = good for setting stop losses.

# Breakers

Easily put, breakers are failed supply and demand order blocks that now act as a flipped level for traders. The most reliable breakers are the ones that offered little to no resistance when previously tested as supply/demand. If it previously was a valid order block, that automatically means the breaker is valid.

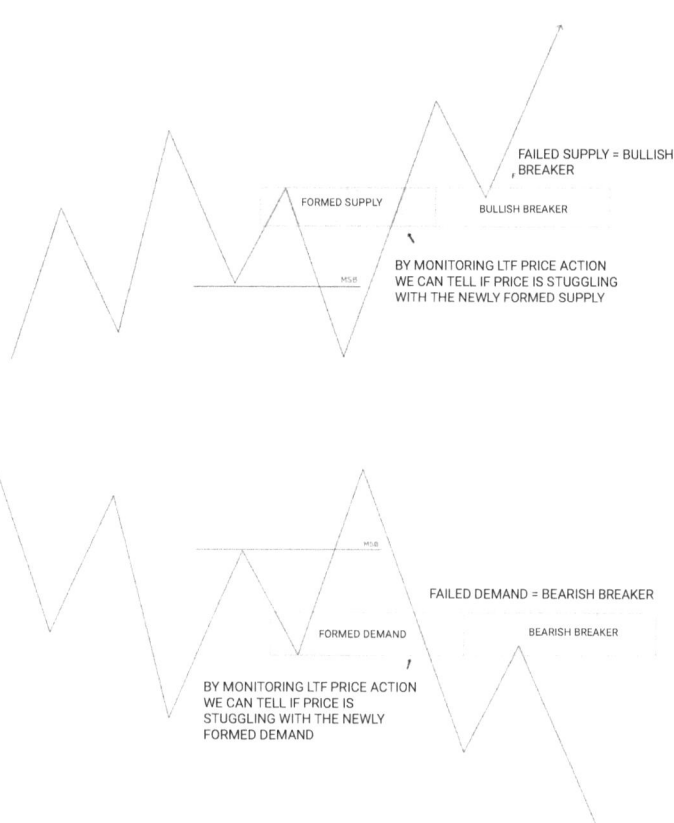

But not all failed order blocks are reliable breakers. How can we find one?

For Bullish Breakers

We find the preceding supply order block. Price must blow through the supply order block, automatically invalidating it and the OB should offer little to no resistance.

If a market structure break occurs after the order block was proven invalid that turns the breaker into a high-interest area. For bullish breakers, a new higher high is made after a previous MSB to the downside. This is optional but it is one of the greatest probability enhancers for breakers.

To execute them you must Set your bids at the top of the order block (now our identified breaker) and place stops below the breaker.

For Bearish Breakers

We find the preceding demand order block. Price must blow through the demand order block, automatically invalidating it and the OB should offer little to no resistance.

To execute them you must set your asks at the bottom of the order block (now our identified breaker) and place stops above the breaker.

If a market structure break occurs after the order block was proven invalid that turns the breaker into a high-interest area.

For bearish breakers: a new lower low is made after a previous MSB to the upside which is optional but it is one of the greatest probability enhancers for breakers.

In the same case as S/D order blocks, breakers can also be proven invalidated. The same principles that govern order blocks apply to breakers:

Again, one of the most recommended things to do is to monitor LTF price action as price approaches the area of interest. If price is showing reversion patterns, that increases the probabilities of our OB to be valid. Therefore, we enter our positions.

To Play Breakers Effectively you have to anticipate them. Weak order blocks tend to offer solid breakers once they are proven invalid.

You should look to play solid S/D order blocks and expect weak S/D order blocks to fail (these tend to trap traders).

To add some context to your chart, if price is within a range you need to ask could this be a deviation? Or is this a stop hunt/trap?

What has been the behaviour of previous price action?

Are traders getting trapped constantly? Or is the asset trending?

To determine the strength of your breaker, assess price action and market conditions.

*Note: If you had a previously valid order block marked out, that probably means that many traders also highlighted that area in their charts. Therefore, as price broke straight through the OB, many traders are now underwater and looking for a retracement to puke their positions and exit the closest they can to break-even.*

# First Obstacles

Price does not always tend to retest S/D order blocks or perfectly flipped highs/levels. Knowing that, we could mark out possible opportunities to join a strong trend by marking the First Obstacles.

A First Obstacle in an uptrend, this is the first resistance after a break of a previous swing high and in a downtrend, this is the first support after a break of a previous swing low.

38

Supply and Demand Clusters

Different to order blocks, these are structures (or candle clusters) that preceded an impulsive move. For them to be valid, you can apply the same criteria as with OB's.

To execute more precise entries, dig into LTF's to find the exact OB you would like to bid/ask.

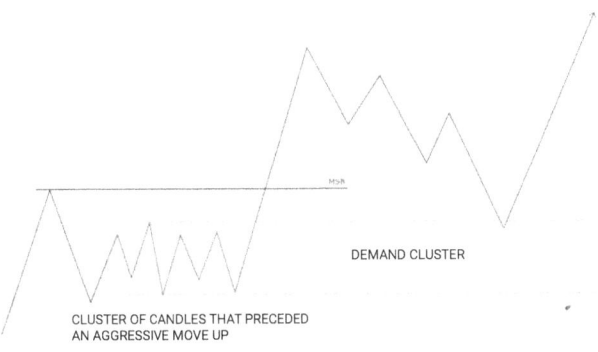

DEMAND CLUSTER

CLUSTER OF CANDLES THAT PRECEDED
AN AGGRESSIVE MOVE UP

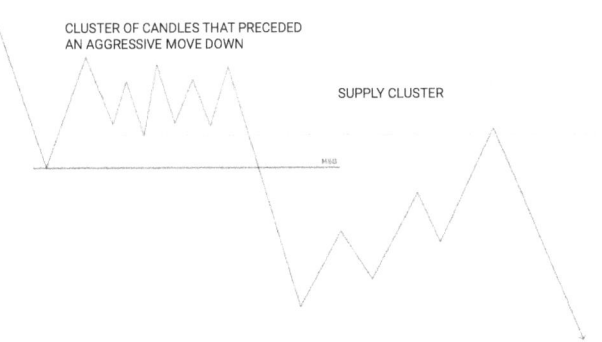

CLUSTER OF CANDLES THAT PRECEDED
AN AGGRESSIVE MOVE DOWN

SUPPLY CLUSTER

# The Timeframe Matrix

Having a directional bias is one of the most useful things you can implement in your strategy. Price may not have the same structure at all timeframes, so a directional bias allows you play in tandem with a HTF trend and knowing what side of the market is being favoured and which isn't. Therefore, having a directional bias enhances your probabilities of succeeding.

When looking at a setup, you want to make sure you are not counter-trend trading. Therefore, at least two timeframes should be pointing in the same direction, it's not about catching perfect bottoms or shorting absolute tops, it's about finding high risk reward plays.

| HTF Structure | Directional Bias TF | Entry TF |
|---|---|---|
| M | W | D1 |
| W | D1 | H4 |
| D1 | H4 | H1 |
| H4 | H1 | M15 |
| H1 | M15 | M5/M3/M1 |

Here is an example on how to implement it

Let's say we have a whole day for ourselves and want to spend the day scalping at home. The steps would be:

1. Determine the HTF Structure, in this case, finding the market structure at the H1 chart.

2. Mark out the key levels at the HTF chart. You don't want to find yourself shorting a 5-minutes supply block when price is approaching a H1 demand order block - timeframes have hierarchy over each other.

3. Determine the Directional Bias structure. In this case, finding the market structure at the M15 chart.

4. Mark out the key levels at the Directional Bias chart. In this case, we would highlight levels from the 15-minutes chart, remember timeframes hierarchy. Look for order blocks, S/R.

5. Execute in your entry timeframe according to your directional bias. If the directional bias is bullish, look for longs. Refine your entries within the M5, M3 and M1 chart. If the directional bias is bearish = look for shorts. Refine your entries within the M5, M3 and m1 chart.

6. And finally happy trading!

*Note: Always be aware of HTF market structure and don't trade against your directional bias, if your directional bias is bullish, you are looking for longs and if your directional bias is bearish, you are looking for shorts.*

# Patterns and Setups

The bullish Quasimodo chart pattern: This appears at the end of a downtrend and indicates a potential reversal to the upside. So, it is like the inverse head and shoulder pattern, consisting of three swing lows, with the middle one being the lowest, and two swing highs, with the second high being significantly higher than the first.

A bearish Quasimodo shows the emergence of a lower swing low and a lower swing high, which are characteristic of a bearish trend, in a previously up-trending market. This shows that a reversal to the downside is likely.

## Over and Under / Quasimodo's

Basically, it consists of shorting the right shoulder of a H&S pattern. In the case of a bullish O/U, longing the right shoulder. You can spot is when:

1. Price finds support or resistance

2. Price breaks through that level, grabbing liquidity
a. Bullish O/U: price breaks up

b. Bearish O/U: price breaks down

3. Price pulls back to retest

4. Price approaches previous support or resistance, depending on the case

5. Enter position placing your SL above/below the "head" of the pattern

# Bearish Quasimodo / Over-and-Under Structure

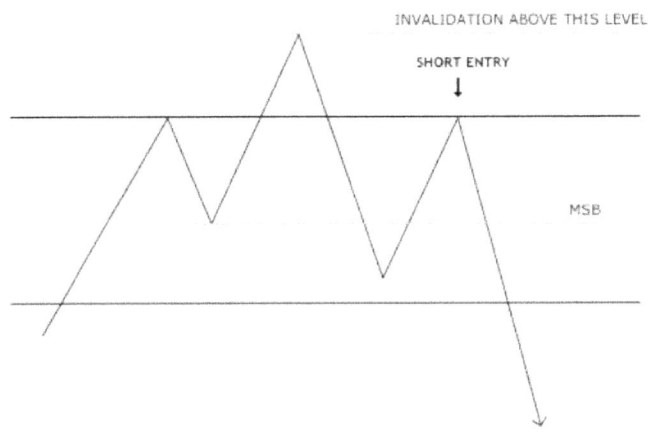

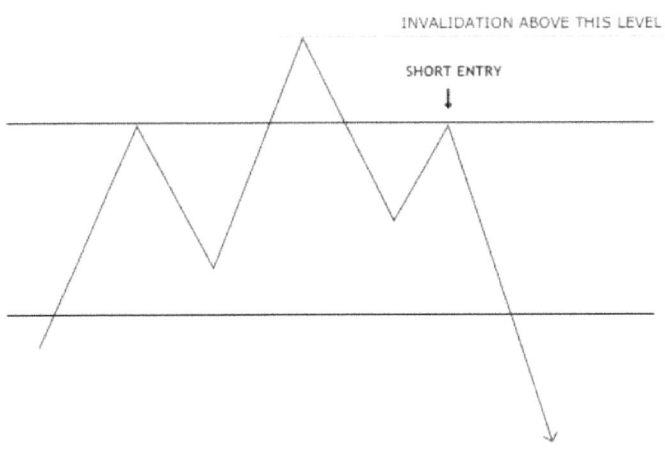

# Bullish Quasimodo / Over-and-Under Structure

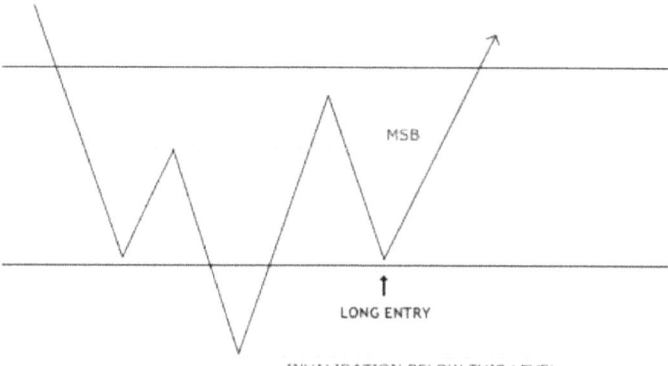

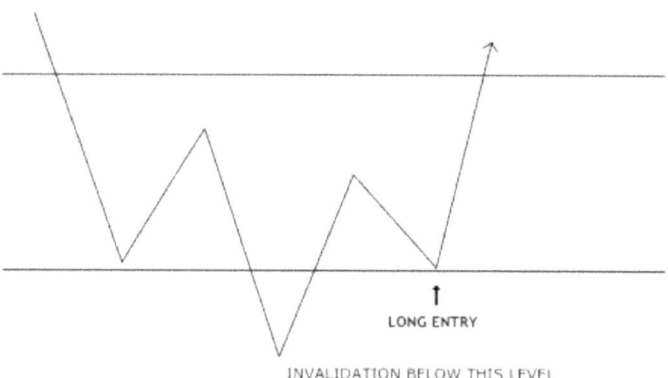

Three Tap or Triple Bottom

The three-tap setup has a high probability rate to predict a visit towards the opposite extreme of a range. It's tailored around trapping breakout traders and forming a base to retest after that (where they puke their positions).

How to spot it?

1. Identify your range

2. After a swing point is swept/deviated, prepare to bid/ask the original range low/high

3. Retest

a. If you anticipated a price retest with bids/asks, place your stops below/above the wick that swept the swing. Very similar to how you'd execute an Over-and-Under

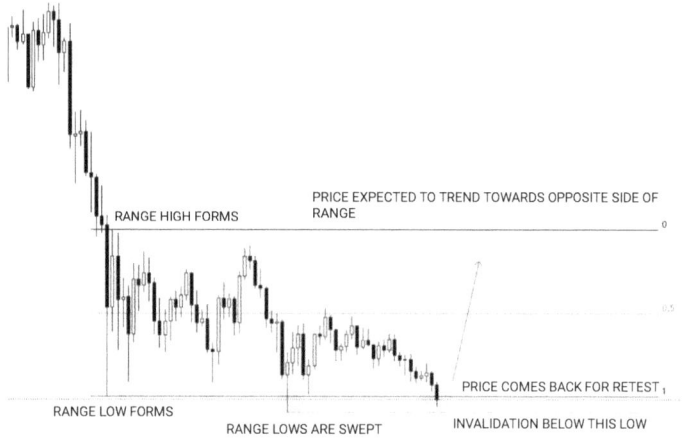

RANGE HIGH FORMS

PRICE EXPECTED TO TREND TOWARDS OPPOSITE SIDE OF RANGE

0

0.5

PRICE COMES BACK FOR RETEST 1

RANGE LOW FORMS

RANGE LOWS ARE SWEPT

INVALIDATION BELOW THIS LOW

RANGE HIGH FORMS

0

0.5

PRICE COMES BACK FOR RETEST 1

RANGE LOW FORMS

RANGE LOWS ARE SWEPT

INVALIDATION BELOW THIS LOW

For a bearish illustration, the opposite happens. Inverted scale for representation.

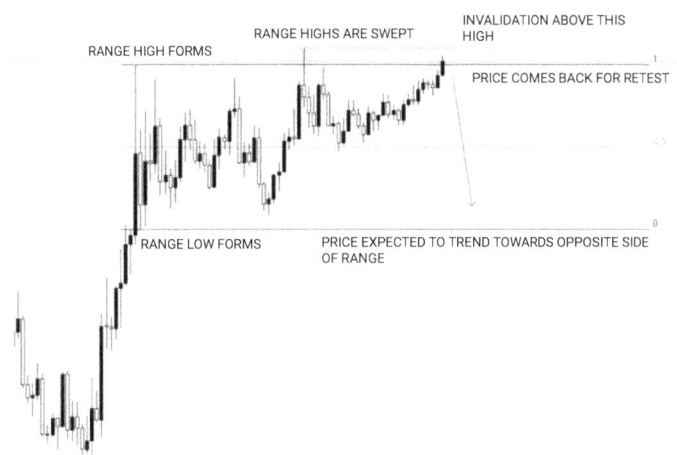

## Swing Failure Pattern (SFP)

A swing failure pattern occurs when a candle trades above/below a significant swing high/low, then fails to close above/below. These are basically failed attempts to break structure.

Bullish SFP - Inverse logic applies to a bearish SFP

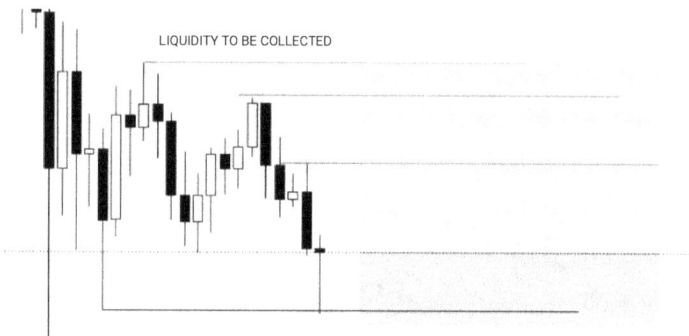

LIQUIDITY TO BE COLLECTED

PRICE TRADES BELOW A SIGNIFICANT WICK (D1 TF)-CONFIRMED BULLISH SFP

WE COULD ENTER A POSITION AIMING TOWARDS THOSE LEVELS OF LIQUIDITY

INVAIDATION BELOW THE WICK

PRICE COLLECTED LIQUIDITY BEFORE BEING REJECTED

2.63R TRADE

PRICE TRADES BELOW A SIGNIFICANT WICK (D1 TF)-CONFIRMED BULLISH SFP

Over-and-Unders, Three Taps and SFP's are setups you can anticipate and execute. Remember, price is always telling a story, is up to you to get hints on what it may do next.

Watch LTF price action behaviour, changes in structure on LTF may give clues to what comes next on HTF.

Some other basic setups include the following:

• Longing demand

• Shorting supply

• Failed demand order block = breaker (look for shorts from this level)

• Failed supply order block = breaker (look for longs from this level)


*Remember that successful price action trading requires practice, discipline, and a thorough understanding of market dynamics. It's essential to develop a trading plan and manage risk effectively to minimize potential losses.*

# Resources and Further Reading

The Trading Geek - YouTube

The Moving Average - YouTube

Rayner Teo - YouTube

MoneyZG - YouTube

Social Media:

*Follow reputable figures in the crypto space on Twitter for real-time updates and insights.*

Online Forums:

*Platforms like Stack Exchange have dedicated sections for blockchain and cryptocurrency related questions.*

# Appendices

Glossary and Terms

EQ = Equilibrium

LTF = Low/Lower Timeframes

HTF = High/higher Timeframes

MSB = Market Structure Break

OB = Order block

S/D = Supply and Demand

SSR = Significant Support/Resistance

S/R = Support and Resistance


Frequently asked questions (FAQs) about price action trading:


1. What is price action trading?

- Price action trading is a strategy where traders analyze and make trading decisions based on the historical and current price movements of an asset, often using candlestick patterns, support and resistance levels, and other visual cues.

2. How does price action differ from other trading strategies?

- Price action trading differs from other strategies because it doesn't rely heavily on technical indicators, oscillators, or fundamental data. Instead, it focuses on interpreting the raw price movement on a chart.

3. What are some common price action patterns?

- Common price action patterns include pin bars, engulfing patterns, doji candles, inside bars, and head and shoulders formations. Traders use these patterns to make decisions about potential price movements.

4. What are support and resistance levels in price action trading?

- Support levels are price points at which an asset tends to find buying interest and move higher. Resistance levels are price points at which an asset faces selling pressure and may move lower. Traders often use these levels to set entry and exit points.

5. Can price action trading be used with other indicators?

- Yes, traders often combine price action analysis with other indicators like moving averages, RSI, and MACD to confirm their trading decisions. However, the primary focus remains on price action.

6. How can I learn price action trading?

- You can learn price action trading through books, online courses, webinars, and practice on trading platforms. It's essential to start with the basics and gradually build your knowledge and skills.

7. Is price action trading suitable for beginners?

- Price action trading can be challenging for beginners because it requires a good understanding of market psychology and the ability to read price charts effectively. However, with dedication and practice, beginners can learn and apply price action strategies.

8. Are there any risks associated with price action trading?

- Like any trading strategy, price action trading carries risks. Traders can still experience losses, and it requires discipline and risk management to be successful. It's essential to have a well-defined trading plan.

9. What timeframes are commonly used in price action trading?

- Price action trading can be applied to various timeframes, from very short-term (e.g., minutes or hours) to longer-term (e.g., daily or weekly). The choice of timeframe depends on your trading style and goals.

10. Can price action trading be used in different markets?

  - Yes, price action trading can be applied to various financial markets, including stocks, forex, commodities, and cryptocurrencies. The principles of price action analysis remain similar across different markets.

*These FAQs can help individuals get started with price action concepts in trading of cryptocurrencies. Remember that the cryptocurrency market is highly dynamic and speculative, so conducting thorough research and risk assessment is crucial before making investment decisions.*

www.ingramcontent.com/pod-product-compliance
Lightning Source LLC
Chambersburg PA
CBHW062257290526
45794CB00006B/2586